YOUR KNOWLEDGE HAS VALUE

- We will publish your bachelor's and master's thesis, essays and papers

- Your own eBook and book - sold worldwide in all relevant shops

- Earn money with each sale

Upload your text at www.GRIN.com
and publish for free

Bibliographic information published by the German National Library:

The German National Library lists this publication in the National Bibliography; detailed bibliographic data are available on the Internet at http://dnb.dnb.de .

This book is copyright material and must not be copied, reproduced, transferred, distributed, leased, licensed or publicly performed or used in any way except as specifically permitted in writing by the publishers, as allowed under the terms and conditions under which it was purchased or as strictly permitted by applicable copyright law. Any unauthorized distribution or use of this text may be a direct infringement of the author s and publisher s rights and those responsible may be liable in law accordingly.

Imprint:

Copyright © 2018 GRIN Verlag
Print and binding: Books on Demand GmbH, Norderstedt Germany
ISBN: 9783668736979

This book at GRIN:

https://www.grin.com/document/430697

Caroline Mutuku

The Impact of new Communication Technology on Unemployment and the increased Gender Inequality

Media, Power and Ethics

GRIN Verlag

GRIN - Your knowledge has value

Since its foundation in 1998, GRIN has specialized in publishing academic texts by students, college teachers and other academics as e-book and printed book. The website www.grin.com is an ideal platform for presenting term papers, final papers, scientific essays, dissertations and specialist books.

Visit us on the internet:

http://www.grin.com/

http://www.facebook.com/grincom

http://www.twitter.com/grin_com

Introduction

Currently, there is a renewed concern regarding the technological advancement that is feared that it may displace much of workforce and consequently create widespread unemployment, human hardship, and social disruption. Some economists have advanced the argument that government must act to avert the loss of jobs that are likely to be replaced by technology. Opposition to technology stems from a lack of understanding of the economic usefulness of technology. The contribution of technology to economic development can only be realized if the new technology is diffused and applied. Diffusion results from the individual's decisions in exploitation of the new technology. The paper will discuss the impact of new communication technology on unemployment and the increased gender inequality and women portrayal in the media.

Communication Technology and Unemployment

The developments of information technology have created a new economy with the digital technology allowing for labor productivity, flexibility and adaptability. Many workplaces have embraced the use of computers and the internet making them normal operating technologies.[1] At a theoretical level, e-commerce has been seen as reducing the coordination costs of the work processes leading to the organizations fragmenting tasks in order to improve the labor productivity. There is a wide integration of information and communication technologies as central to the creation of the new global knowledge-based enterprises which plays an important role in facilitating the growth and promoting the sustainable development.[2] Economically, information technology is supposed to be the driving force that engages the global transformation of the global economy. In regular language, technology advancement refers to some changes that allow the production of more goods and services. The connotation meaning centers on the exploitation of machines such as computers, however, any more efficient way of production is a technological advancement. Technological advancement also leads to an increase of better living standards which results from greater output and more leisure.[3]

The information age is a new phenomenon that has brought with it new challenges as the people seek to integrate the expanding universe of multimedia in their daily lives. The term

---

1. Brynjolfsson, E. and McAfee, A. *The race against the machine: how the digital revolution is accelerating innovation, driving productivity, and irreversibly transforming employment and the economy*, Lexington: Digital frontier press, 2011. p. 15.
2. Brynjolfsson and McAfee, p. 20.
3. Castells, Manuel. *The Rise of the Network Society: The Information Age: Economy, Society, and Culture*, Hoboken: John Wiley & Sons, 2011, p. 26.

Information is often used to describe a cybernetic community where there is a greater dependence on the use of computers and related data transmission linkages to create and transmit information. The regular reference to an industrial society relied on the use of machinery to augment the human physical labor in production. Presently, through a process of continuous change, geographical barriers have been broken, business more interconnected, and the relations between the workers and their workplace are rapidly changing.[4] From a technological perspective, the new media technological innovations have presented a new system of communication, networking, and inter-linkages that have revolutionized the way business and communication operate. Consequently, from an information perspective, the new media innovations can be seen in the generation, access, and exploitation as well as sharing of information. Some scholars have suggested that the new media portends some kind of technological determinism where the effects are determined by technology growth rather than the social networks that influenced their development.[5] Thus, the media discussions that surround the new media are to be expected since the technological phenomena has brought economic and social change that has redefined the traditional media messages, audiences, and channels while replacing them with new processes of communication. Consequently, it is impossible to separate the process of communication as envisaged in new media from technology since it operates in the public sphere by utilizing technology. The first part of the paper discusses the effect of new media technology on employment or unemployment while the second part addresses the increased gender inequality in the use of media.

Some scholars have opined that the increased pace of technological development can create two profound side effects in the labor market. New technology can increase the rate of and the average duration of unemployment. Many organizations are likely to view it as cost-effective to retrain some workers in order to keep up with new technological change. These are likely to be the less educated and older employees.[6] The net effects would be prolonged duration of unemployment while some of them never working again. Thus, the level of unemployment will increase. However, it has been observed that while technology eliminates jobs, it also creates jobs. It is pervasive in destroying the lower wage and low productivity jobs while it also creates jobs that are more productive and high skilled, and consequently, more rewarding. Historically, the power of creating better income through technological innovations has proven

---

4. Castells, p. 32.
5. Salvadori, Neri Balducci, Renato. *Innovation, Unemployment, and Policy in the Theories of Growth and Distribution,* Northampton: Edward Elgar Publishing, 2005. p. 53.
6. Salvadori, Neri Balducci, Renato. *Innovation, Unemployment, and Policy in the Theories of Growth and Distribution,* Northampton: Edward Elgar Publishing, 2005. p. 53.

to be more powerful than its labor displacing effects.⁷ Thus, scholars observe that the technological development has always been accompanied by higher output and higher overall employment. Technological development allows the society to get more output from the existing resources. The technological advances may be less costly methods of production or may result in the production of new and improved commodities. Consequently, the society gains from more output and highly valued commodities.⁸

Historically, technological development or change has resulted in the increase of labor demands in some labor markets and a decrease of labor demands in other labor markets. For instance, the introduction of the assembly line form of production and the production of interchangeable parts increased in labor productivity. The innovation also led to an increase on the demand for unskilled workers while decreasing the demand for skilled artisans.⁹ In the same vein of observation, the coming of automated production processes resulted in the decrease of the demand for unskilled labor while increasing the demand for quality control technicians and skilled computer programmers. Suffice to say, technological innovation will always alter the composition of the labor market demand. It creates demand for some types of labor and decreases the demand for other types of labor.¹⁰

Although the introduction of new technology may adversely affect the demand for labor in some categories of the labor markets, the net effect of the technological innovation on the total employment scenario may be positive because it tends to increase the rate of economic growth. Economists have opined that high rates of economic growth are associated with reduced unemployment rates.¹¹ The relationship that exist between the economic growth and the changes in the employments dynamics is illustrated in the Okun's law which claims that a one percent growth reduces the unemployment rate by a third of the one percent. Although there may be some doubts on the overall magnitude of the effect, there is enough empirical evidence that unemployment is reduced by the increased economic growth.¹²

---

7 . Salvadori and Balducci, p. 56.

8 . Castells, Manuel. *The Rise of the Network Society: The Information Age: Economy, Society, and Culture,* Hoboken: John Wiley & Sons, 2011, p. 3.

9 . Frey, Carl and Osborne Michael, 2013. *The future of employment: how susceptible are jobs to computerization?* p. 6. http://www.oxfordmartin.ox.ac.uk/downloads/academic/The_Future_of_Employment.pdf
10 . IbidFry and Osborne, . p. 8
11 . Salvadori, Neri Balducci, Renato. *Innovation, Unemployment, and Policy in the Theories of Growth and Distribution,* Northampton: Edward Elgar Publishing, 2005. p. 49.
12 . Salvadori and Balducci, p. 52.

In the last few decades, computers have been used to substitute a number of tasks such as telephone operators, bookkeepers, and cashiers. In the recent past; however, the poor performance of labor market in the advanced economies has rekindled the discussion on technological unemployment. Some scholars have given the computer controlled equipments as a contributor to the rising rates of unemployment.[13] The effects of computerization on jobs outcomes has been observed through the study of the decline on employment mostly in routine intensive works, such as jobs consisting of tasks that follow well-defined processes that can be achieved by sophisticated algorithms. For instance, some scholars have emphasized the decline in manufacturing employment is the cause o the current low rate of employment. Additionally, the effect of computerization can be observed in the structural shift with workers reallocating the labor supply from middle-income industries to low-income service occupations.[14] It has been argued that the manual jobs in the service industry are less susceptible to computerization since they need flexibility and physical adaptability. However, Brynjolfsson and McAfee (2011) have observed that technological innovations are on the increase with development of more sophisticated technologies, and hence, disrupting the labor markets and making many employees redundant.[15] On the other hand, with the cost of computing coming down, the problem-solving skills are viewed as becoming productive, which explains the substantial employment growth in jobs that require cognitive skills. The growth of information technologies in their diverse forms such as e-commerce and the internet has revolutionized the labor market.[16] The new technology has become integral elements of commerce, industry, and business, consequently driving of the modern economy.

Increased Gender Inequality in Use of Media

In the age of technology, many people come in contact with media on a daily basis. People are regularly bombarded with information; hence, the media acquire powerful influences on the individual thoughts. The messages and information sent out through the media are in the interests of those who control the messages. Thus, in regard to the gender inequality in the use of media, the messages are based on the superiority of the male gender that control and dominate the industry. Women are oppressed through marginalization and objectification

---

13 . Brynjolfsson, E. and McAfee, A. *The race against the machine: how the digital revolution is accelerating innovation, driving productivity, and irreversibly transforming employment and the economy*, Lexington: Digital frontier press, 2011. p. 61.
14 .Brynjolfsson and McAfee. p. 64.
15 . Salvadori, Neri and Balducci, Renato. *Innovation, Unemployment, and Policy in the Theories of Growth and Distribution*, Northampton: Edward Elgar Publishing, 2005. p. 86.
16 . Salvadori and Balducci, p. 89.

so that men can retain the privilege, social power, and opportunities.[17] The oppression is predominantly committed the gendered white male who power and therefore control the means of communication such as the media. A look at the television shows and advertisements shows that the underlying theme as portrayed by those in power is that women are less competent, deceitful, promiscuous, and preoccupied with trivialities. The media also shape the society's perception of how a woman is supposed to look. Through the clever digital manipulation of the women on the adverts and the increased use of thin models, a false and unattainable form of the ideal woman is made; therefore, for those women who do not fit within the unattainable mold, pressure is mounted so that they can adjust to the ideal woman image.[18] Additionally, the blatant control of women is internalized by the society and hence, the perpetuated for generations. Most people now have access and are increasingly relying on the internet and related forms of media as their source of information and what is projected by the media must be scrutinized through a critical eye. The study of sociology reveals several theoretical levels that discuss the possible causes and potential solutions to these social problems.[19]

Conflict theory shows that people are in a never ending battle for resources and power. Consequently, viewing the influence of the media on gender inequality through the conflict theory, the prevalence of the gender bias can be explained. According to the conflict theorists, the problem in the media is to be traced to the convergence of ownership.[20] The media are controlled by a small clique of people and the products thereof are likely to be partial to the people who control the source of the products. The conflict theorist also observe that gender inequality is the result of the tight control of the means of production and deliberate subjugation of women through social institutions, consequently, it is men who hold the positions of power and it is to their interest to portray women in the media negative and marginalized manner so as to maintain the societal control.[21] Most of the mainstream media adopt stereotyping as the standard way of casting the people. Thus, in the media, leading women characters are presented as overwhelmed by their roles and responsibilities. The other portrayal is of deceit;

---

17. Gill, Rosaling. *Gender and the Media,* Cambridge: Polity, 2007. P. 22.
18. European Commission. 2010. *Opinion on "Breaking Gender Stereotypes in the Media".* p. 4.
http://ec.europa.eu/justice/genderequality/files/opinions_advisory_committee/2010_12_opinion_on_breaking_gender_stereotypes_in_the_media_en.pdf

19. Gill, Rosaling. *Gender and the Media,* Cambridge: Polity, 2007. p. 24.
20. European Commission. 2010. *Opinion on "Breaking Gender Stereotypes in the Media".* p. 6.
http://ec.europa.eu/justice/genderequality/files/opinions_advisory_committee/2010_12_opinion_on_breaking_gender_stereotypes_in_the_media_en.pdf
21. Gill, p. 26

consequently, women characters who occupy positions of power; and they regularly engage in irresponsible and deceitful behaviors.

The media, despite the profound changes on the media landscapes and the influential role the media market plays in content development and management; it is still regarded as the fourth estate.[22] Despite the dominance of the consumer-oriented discourse in the media; a discourse that characterizes communication as a business, it is the fundamental and democratic principle that guides the public policy expectations in accordance with the instruments and international standards of human rights. The role of the media in gender democracy has been of concern for a long time when juxtaposed with process of trying to gain gender equality. In the media, the role is identified in the representation of gender and antecedent roles in design, production, and content programming where the media reinforces the gender stereotypes and prejudices in regard to women.[23] The role is also reinforced through the structures of the media organizations where women are still a minority in media professions where they are underrepresented either in content production or decision-making positions.

The digital technologies role in shaping people's relation to the media can be explored and understood through the digital rights and policies. The media deregulation has intensified the distribution of sexist content and images of women with the intent to sexualize women and girls. The practice is driven by need to construct marketing niche that rely on the cultivation of the gender roles. Thus, the sexualization of pop culture has been adopted as a standard marketing strategy. It is, therefore, not surprising that elements of pornification has become part of the mainstream media culture as represented in advertising, fashion, and music promotion.[24] These activities are increasingly being influenced and take visual and verbal cues from the lurid pornographic content. However, women are not a homogenous entity with similar experiences; however, they share some intersectionality experiences in multiple and varying degrees of marginalization that could also change from one context to another.[25] The element of intersectionality introduces some difficulties when discussing women in general; however, it forces people to understand the complexity the antecedent challenges facing women.

---

22 . Gll, p. 32.
23 . European Commission. 2010. *Opinion on "Breaking Gender Stereotypes in the Media".* p. 6. http://ec.europa.eu/justice/genderequality/files/opinions_advisory_committee/2010_12_opinion_on_breaking_gender_stereotypes_in_the_media_en.pdf

24 . Gill, Rosaling. *Gender and the Media,* Cambridge: Polity, 2007. p. 32.

25 . European Commission, p. 11.

Conclusion

To sum up, new media technologies have been seen to have positive and negative impacts on people, whether in job creation and destruction or in enhancing the women stereotypes perpetuated by the male dominance in the media industry. It is most likely that new media will continue to perpetuate the stereotypical portrayal of women since it is difficult for governmental authorities to control and regulate the industry.

References

Brynjolfsson, E. and McAfee, A. *The race against the machine: how the digital revolution is accelerating innovation, driving productivity, and irreversibly transforming employment and the economy,* Lexington: Digital frontier press, 2011.

Castells, Manuel. *The Rise of the Network Society: The Information Age: Economy, Society, and Culture,* Hoboken: John Wiley & Sons, 2011.

European Commission. 2010. *Opinion on "Breaking Gender Stereotypes in the Media".* http://ec.europa.eu/justice/genderequality/files/opinions_advisory_committee/2010_12_opinion_on_breaking_gender_stereotypes_in_the_media_en.pdf

Frey, Carl and Osborne Michael, 2013. *The future of employment: how susceptible are jobs to computerization?*
http://www.oxfordmartin.ox.ac.uk/downloads/academic/The_Future_of_Employment.pdf

Gill, Rosaling. *Gender and the Media*, Cambridge: Polity, 2007.

Salvadori, Neri Balducci, Renato. *Innovation, Unemployment, and Policy in the Theories of Growth and Distribution*, Northampton: Edward Elgar Publishing, 2005.

YOUR KNOWLEDGE HAS VALUE

- We will publish your bachelor's and master's thesis, essays and papers

- Your own eBook and book - sold worldwide in all relevant shops

- Earn money with each sale

Upload your text at www.GRIN.com and publish for free